DIG AND DISCOVER
QUARTZ

T0025419

by Melissa Mayer

CAPSTONE PRESS
a capstone imprint

Published by Capstone Press, an imprint of Capstone
1710 Roe Crest Drive, North Mankato, Minnesota 56003
capstonepub.com

Library of Congress Cataloging-in-Publication Data is available on the Library of Congress website
ISBN: 9781666342680 (hardcover)
ISBN: 9781666342703 (paperback)
ISBN: 9781666342710 (ebook PDF)

Summary: Quartz is a mineral found in all types of rocks. It forms a variety of crystals. Uncover how this common mineral gets its many shapes and where you can find it.

All internet sites appearing in back matter were available and accurate when this book was sent to press.

This book provides information about various types of rocks and where and how to find them. Before entering any area in search of rocks, make sure that the area is open to the public or that you have secured permission from the property owner to go there. Also, take care not to damage any property, and do not remove any rocks from the area unless you have permission to do so.

Rock hunting in riverbeds, quarries, mines, and some of the other areas identified in this book can be inherently risky. You should not engage in any of these activities without parental supervision. Also, you should always wear proper safety equipment and know how to use any tools that you bring with you. You should not engage in any activity that is beyond your ability or skill or comfort level. Failure to follow these guidelines may result in damage to property or serious injury or death to you or others, and may also result in substantial civil or criminal liability.

The publisher and the author shall not be liable for any damages allegedly arising from the information in this book, and they specifically disclaim any liability from the use or application of any of the contents of this book.

CONTENTS

Words in **bold** are in the glossary.

INTRODUCTION
ROCKHOUNDING? OF QUARTZ!

Imagine standing at the edge of a creek. Hard, smooth rocks poke your bare feet. Now picture yourself on a beach. Imagine feeling the tiny grains of sand between your toes.

Rocks and sand are often made of quartz. They are part of Earth's **crust**. Scientists who study Earth's crust are **geologists**. But geology isn't just for scientists!

Rock hounds collect rocks, **gems**, **minerals**, and fossils for fun. It's a hobby that took off in the 1930s. The U.S. government began building many roads and bridges. All that digging revealed beautiful rocks. Some people began collecting them. Some polished them to make jewelry.

Quartz can be enjoyed natural or polished.

CHAPTER 1
ALL ABOUT QUARTZ

Have you ever broken a rock in half and spotted sparkly bits inside it? Those are minerals. Rocks are usually mixtures of different minerals.

Minerals are natural but have never been alive. They don't come from plants or animals. They form when the right **elements** come together in the right way—like following a recipe.

There are three basic kinds of rocks. Igneous rocks form when melted rock called magma or lava cools and hardens. Sedimentary rocks form when layers of minerals and debris stack together like lasagna. With enough pressure or heat, both types of rocks can change into metamorphic rocks. Quartz is a mineral found in all three kinds of rock!

Quartz is a popular mineral to add to a rock collection.

Clear quartz may look like glass, but it is stronger. Quartz can scratch glass.

Meet Quartz!

Quartz is one of the most common minerals in the world. Twenty percent of Earth's crust is quartz! Quartz is a main mineral in mountain peaks. It doesn't wear away like other minerals. Beaches and deserts also have tons of quartz.

Quartz forms when the elements silicon and oxygen in the ground mix with heat and water in the right way. This can happen in rock cracks or in superhot water just under Earth's crust. When it cools and hardens, some quartz forms **crystals**.

Pure quartz is clear. Sometimes other elements mix in with the quartz when it's forming. These change its color. Many gems are quartz. They include amethyst, aventurine, citrine, rose quartz, and smoky quartz.

Fantastic Find!

Quartz is common, but pure quartz is rare. One of the few places you can find it is Goiás, a state in Brazil. That's where miners unearthed the biggest quartz crystal ever found. It weighed more than 44 tons. That's as heavy as 22 cars!

Tiny Crystals

Some types of quartz form large crystals. These include amethyst and rose quartz. Other quartz has layers of crystals so tiny you need a microscope to see them. Some examples are agate, jasper, and flint. If you look at sand under a microscope, it's mostly teensy quartz crystals!

Layers of tiny crystals and other elements can make stripes or swirls in agate and jasper. You can polish these to bring out their patterns. Quartz is easy to polish because it's strong and won't crumble.

FACT

Ancient humans used flint to make tools and start fires. Some of the oldest human fossils ever found had flint tools buried with them. They could be 350,000 years old!

Jasper's unique and vibrant patterns make it popular for jewelry.

Quartz sand has many uses.

Quartz Around Your Home

You probably use something made with quartz every day! Playgrounds and sports fields use quartz sand. Companies use quartz sand to make glass, metal, rubber, and paint. That sand is also put on railroad tracks to help trains grip the rails!

If you zap quartz with electricity, it vibrates in a very precise way. That makes it great for keeping time. Quartz watches have parts that track the vibrations to count seconds, minutes, and hours. Those vibrations make quartz great for other tools too.

Microscopes and telescopes rely on quartz. It's used in televisions, gaming systems, computers, and cell phones.

Scientists grow quartz in labs now so they can get the right quality needed for electronics. They drop tiny quartz crystals into a mineral mixture. Then a machine mimics the intense heat and pressure deep inside Earth. The quartz crystals grow!

FACT FILE

Name: quartz
Common types: agate, amethyst, aventurine, citrine, flint, jasper, rose quartz, smoky quartz
Color: clear, purple, green, yellow, orange, pink, gray
Chemical formula: SiO_2 (silicon dioxide)
Found: all over the world in all kinds of rocks (igneous, metamorphic, sedimentary)
Hardness: 7 out of 10 on the Mohs scale (a scale that measures rock hardness from softest to hardest)
Uses: gemstone, glassmaking, collecting natural gas, sand, scientific instruments, watches, and electronics

CHAPTER 2
QUARTZ, QUARTZ EVERYWHERE

Quartz is everywhere. You can find it in gravel. It might be in your neighborhood!

The quartz you find probably won't look like sparkling crystals at first. A lot of unpolished quartz looks like lumpy, white rocks. The key to spotting it is knowing that it's **translucent**. Some light can pass through quartz. The crystal almost seems to glow.

Train your eyes to scan the ground. Look for rocks that seem to shine or glow. Carry a spray bottle of water. Wet the gravel to look for glowing quartz. Hold rocks up to a flashlight to see if light shines through them.

Knowing how light passes through quartz can help you find crystals.

Agates

You can find agates in places with gravel. But one of the best places to look for them is the beach. Many agates show up on the shores of the Pacific Ocean and the Great Lakes. You can also find them in the deserts of the western United States.

Like other quartz, agates seem to glow. They're usually no bigger than your eyeball. Thanks to layers of tiny crystals, they may have colorful stripes or swirls. Some agates have patterns that look like moss, smoke, bubbles, or even monster eyes!

Agates found at the beach may be shiny and smooth. Waves churn them against the sand. They can also look waxy or rough. They may even appear to have a potato-like skin.

Some people enjoy collecting agates for their unique patterns.

CHAPTER 3
ROCKHOUNDING PREP

You've decided to become a rock hound. First, learn everything you can about rocks and minerals. To get the best info, check quality books, websites, and apps. Look at resources put out by colleges or geology organizations. State and national park services are also good sources.

Every rock hound needs a field guide. This will help you identify rocks and minerals. Field guides can be books or apps.

Rock hounds can learn from one another. You can join a rockhounding club or start one yourself. You can ask adults to connect you with a local geologist. Most colleges have geology experts. Some colleges host events for people interested in rockhounding.

Knowing where to start your search and what rocks look like in their natural state will help you identify them.

Gear Up!

Good gear takes rockhounding to the next level. A sturdy backpack with pockets helps you carry gear and rocks. You can also use a bucket or an old lunch box.

Geology hammers can help you safely unearth quartz.

A geology hammer has a blunt side and a sharp side. It works well for digging out quartz. It's easy to lose a hammer while rockhounding. Some people paint their hammers bright colors. If you plan to dig, don't forget a small shovel. You can also use garden tools.

Safety gear is important. Wear sturdy shoes or boots. Put on safety goggles anytime you use tools. Bring a cell phone and compass in case you get lost. Pack work gloves, sunscreen, and a first aid kit. Don't forget water, snacks, and a notebook for field notes.

Take the High Road

Rock hounds should collect carefully. Take only rocks and minerals you love. Fill in any holes you dig. Never leave trash behind. Look for signs and avoid off-limits areas. Always go with an adult.

Make sure you know the rules for collecting rocks before you start gathering them.

Ask permission before taking rocks from private property. The U.S. Forest Service usually allows collecting on its lands. You may need a permit if you want to dig. Cities and states will have their own rules for land they manage. Never collect on the land of an **Indigenous** community you don't belong to.

If you find something amazing, report it to the land manager. Your find could help scientists studying the area!

Fantastic Find!

In 2020, miners working at the border of Brazil and Uruguay cracked open a giant rock and found a surprise. The amethyst geode inside was a perfect heart shape! The geode with the surrounding stone is very heavy, weighing more than 150 pounds (68 kilograms).

You'll need to stay focused in order to find quartz along the ground.

Oh, the Places You Will Go

Look for quartz in places where the ground is cut. This could be a dry stream or riverbed cut by water. Comb rocky beaches for agates. You may have good luck right after a storm churns the sand.

You can search online for quartz sites near you. Some private places let you dig rocks and minerals for a fee. Remember that your safety is the real treasure. Never go into water, caves, or mines.

Fantastic Find!

Workers in Austria found a massive vein of amethyst in the 1840s. The glittery purple deposit is at least 1,300 feet (400 meters) long and up to 3.2 feet (1 m) thick. It is 280 million years old! A museum was built around part of the vein.

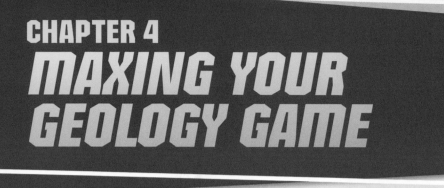

CHAPTER 4
MAXING YOUR GEOLOGY GAME

When you get your treasures home, you'll want to clean them. Use soapy water and a soft toothbrush to remove any dirt.

A field guide will help you identify your find. Some apps let you upload a photo. The apps then suggest possible matches. You can use a book or look online to help confirm the identity of your rock.

FACT

In 1971, astronauts found a rock containing quartz on the moon. But it wasn't really a moon rock. Scientists think it formed on Earth 4 billion years ago. Then an asteroid hit Earth and blasted the rock up to the moon.

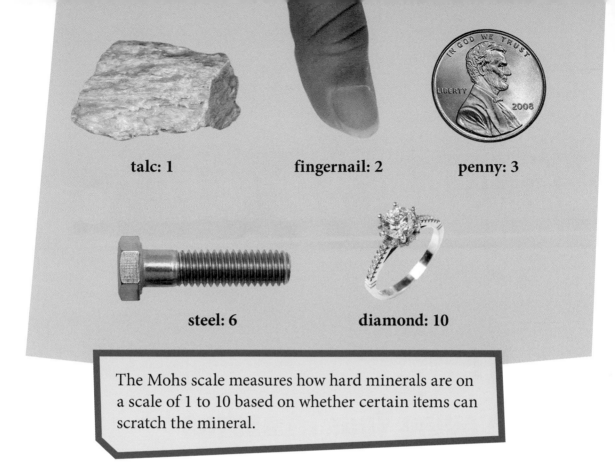

talc: 1   fingernail: 2   penny: 3

steel: 6   diamond: 10

The Mohs scale measures how hard minerals are on a scale of 1 to 10 based on whether certain items can scratch the mineral.

The Mohs hardness scale tells how hard a rock or mineral is. This helps you identify different minerals. You can use common objects to figure this out. If you can scratch it, it's softer than the object you used to scratch it.

Quartz is a 7 on the Mohs scale. A steel nail won't even scratch it. You can buy a Mohs scale testing kit. The minerals in a kit are labeled with their hardness so you can use them to scratch and compare.

A magnifying glass can help you admire your collection up close.

Enjoying Your Treasures

Don't forget to take good notes! Document when and where you find your treasures. Write down what kind of quartz you find. Note its size, shape, color, and texture. This will help you keep track of each item in your collection.

The shiny rocks and minerals sold in stores are polished. To polish your finds at home, you'll need a rock tumbler. This is a machine you fill with sand or grit. It works like the tides on a beach, rolling the rocks against the sand until they're smooth. This takes several weeks.

Keep only the rocks and minerals you love. There are lots of choices for showing them off. Display them in a glass jar, an egg carton, a cardboard box, or a tackle box. Show them to family and friends. Maybe they will get interested in rockhounding too!

Are you ready to dig into rock hunting? There may be treasures just outside your door!

CRYSTAL CATALOG

DATE FOUND	QUARTZ TYPE	SIZE	COLOR	DESCRIPTION	LOCATION
6/1/2021	agate	2 x 1 centimeters	brown with black spots	round, egg-shaped	McKenzie River, Oregon
7/24/2022	jasper	1.3 x 0.6 cm	spotted yellow and red	oval with one end chipped off	Quartzville Creek, Oregon

GLOSSARY

crust (KRUHST)—the outer layer of Earth, which is made of rocks and minerals

crystal (KRI-stul)—a solid substance having a regular pattern, often with many flat surfaces

element (EH-luh-muhnt)—a substance that cannot be broken down into simpler substances

gem (JEM)—a precious stone often used in jewelry

geologist (jee-AH-luh-jist)—a scientist who studies the physical Earth, including rocks and minerals

Indigenous (in-DIH-juh-nuhs)—relating to people who lived in a place first

mineral (MIN-ur-uhl)—a substance found in nature that is not made by a plant or animal

rock hound (ROK HAUND)—someone who looks for and collects rocks as a hobby

translucent (trans-LOO-suhnt)—not fully see-through, but able to let some light pass through

READ MORE

Dickmann, Nancy. *Dig and Discover Agates*. North Mankato, MN: Capstone, 2023.

Sawyer, Ava. *Sedimentary Rocks*. North Mankato, MN: Capstone, 2019.

Tomecek, Steve. *Rockopedia*. Washington, DC: National Geographic Kids, 2020.

INTERNET SITES

American Federation of Mineralogical Societies Future Rockhounds of America: Roster of Participating Clubs
amfed.org/kids.htm

National Geographic Kids: Geology 101
kids.nationalgeographic.com/science/article/geology-101

Wonderopolis: Where Does the Sand on Beaches Come From?
wonderopolis.org/wonder/Where-Does-the-Sand-on-Beaches-Come-From

INDEX

ABOUT THE AUTHOR

Melissa Mayer is a science writer and former science teacher who's currently working on an MS in Entomology. She lives on a tiny urban homestead in Portland, Oregon, with her wife, kids, and way too many animals—dogs, cats, rabbits, chickens, and an ever-growing collection of insects. She's the author of nonfiction books for children and young adults.

Editorial Credits
Editor: Marie Pearson; Designer: Joshua Olson; Production Specialists: Joshua Olson and Polly Fisher

Image Credits
Alamy: volkerpreusser, 25; Getty Images: aamorim, 22; Shutterstock: Anna Kucherova, 20, emrahyazicioglu, Bottom Right 27, Epitavi, Bottom 5, indigolotos, 11, Jacob Boomsma, 17, jopelka, Cover, 1, Kues, (texture) design element throughout, Leestudio, Top Middle 27, Marco Fine, Top 5, Mega Pixel, Bottom Left 27, Minakryn Ruslan, Top Left 27, Nyura, 28, Oveskyfly, 8, Pedal to the Stock, 19, pzAxe, 12, Spiroview Inc, Top Right 27, Stefan Malloch, 7, Volodymyr Dvornyk, 15, Yes058 Montree Nanta, 24